A FISHERMAN'S NIGHT BEFORE
Christmas

Text
Steve Stovall

Jody Feldman

Illustrations
Shauna Mooney Kawasaki

GIBBS-SMITH

03 02 01 00   10 9 8 7 6 5

Copyright © 1995 Gibbs Smith, Publisher

Printed in Hong Kong
by Regent Publishing Services, Ltd.

Published by
Gibbs Smith, Publisher
P. O. Box 667
Layton, Utah 84041

ISBN 0-87905-681-9

'Twas the night
before Christmas
on a big lake
"down East,"

anglers fished
in their shanties
with dreams
of a feast.

O'er auger-drilled
ice holes,
they sat and
they knelt

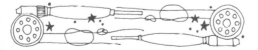

in hopes of
a big catch
of perch, pike,
and smelt.

Just then,
a jalopy-like
sleigh fell
from space,

strewing buckets
of minnows
all over the place.

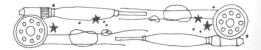

Then out popped
old Santa.
"I need help,
I fear.

"Every letter
before me
says, 'Send
fishing gear!'

"I've requests
from all over,
and I'm running
quite late,

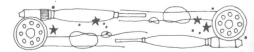

" 'cause I don't
know my rigs
and my lures
from my bait."

They laughed
and then said,
"Well, for that type
of haul,

we'll just
catalog shop,
then give
Bass Pro a call.

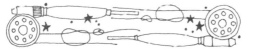

Making Santa's
selections,
they used his
charge card,

then flew off
to the store
and found gifts
by the yard:

For largemouth!
For salmon!
For muskies!
And splake!

For walleyes!
For sunnies!
For mackerel!
And hake!

Some waders
for rivers!
Some flippers!
Some floats!

Some inboards!
Some outboards!
Some motors
for boats!

They even picked
fly rods
and sleek
spinning reels,

tied flies by
the dozens,
and plenty
of creels.

The sleigh
was now loaded
with poles, jigs,
and plugs,

with spoons and
bright lures
that resembled
big bugs.

"It's great!"
Santa said,
"I can't thank
you enough.

"But I have
one more problem:
just who gets
which stuff?"

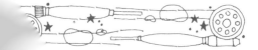

So Santa's
new helpers
climbed back on
the sleigh.

"Take off,
and we'll give you
some lessons
today."

They flew off
to Montauk
and Jersey's shoreline;

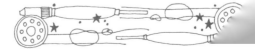

Carolina locales
hidden deep
in the pine.

Wherever
they flew,
they gave just
the right gear.

They flew east!
They flew west!
They flew far!
They flew near!

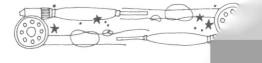

Then,
off to Mobile
with its catfish
and gar,

and up the
Gulf Coast
where great
bullheads are.

They expressed
some concern
for those guys
in the Keys,

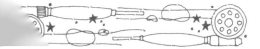

'cause bone-fish
fanatics
are harder
to please.

Then, north toward
the border
for smallmouth
and trout,

where muskies
and pickerel
swim all about.

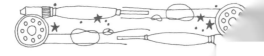

Down Yellowstone way,
heading toward
Jackson Hole;

to the
Grand Tetons next—
they were reaching
their goal.

Where rivers
run through
it—Great Falls
to Big Sky—

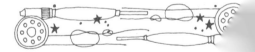

they pointed
out steelhead
you just catch
and fry.

They stopped
at all points
from Wasatch
to Sun Valley,

dropping tackle
and bait
but with no time
to dally.

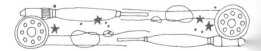

For just as the
Washington
salmon were
spawning,

dawn hinted
of breaking,
and Santa
was yawning.

One last stop
in Frisco —
red snapper
for all.

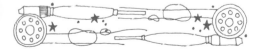

Santa said,
fork in hand,
"Now I'm having
a ball."

With their bellies
all full,
back to Maine
Santa flew,

giving bobbers
and gaffs
to each one
of his crew.

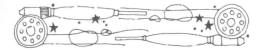

Soon they heard
him exclaim
as he drove
out of sight,

"Happy Christmas
to all!
May the fish
always bite!"